Beltain
May 1st
Litha
June 21st
Lammas
August 2nd
Mabon
September 21st
Samhain
October 31st
Yule
December 21st
Imbolc
February 2nd
Oestara
March 21st

Copyright MorningStar Publishers

All rights reserved. No part of this book may be reproduced without written permission of the copyright owner, except for the use of limited quotations for the purpose of book reviews.

NAME_____
    _____

The Wheel of the Year

Samhain

Forward

This pamphlet will provide a good understanding of Samhain, the first of the eight Festivals of the Wheel of the Year and the way it is celebrated. Each of the eight festival have been extracted from the guide book, <u>'The Wheel of the Year. A beginners guide to celebrating the traditional pagan festivals of the year.'</u> New suggestions on your celebrations available only in these pamphlets have been added. If you are new to the Craft this selection of pamphlets will give you a solid base from where you can increase your understanding of the Craft and its many branches. For the more knowledgeable they will provide tried and tested ways to celebrate each of the eight Sabbats of the Wheel in a meaningful and fulfilling way other than in a formal Circle.

Included in each pamphlet are lists of correspondences, guided meditation, spells and seasonal activities linked to the festival. They have been crafted to resonate with the influences of the season and are the result of many years of personal celebration of The Wheel. Although I have worked within a group, my true path lies as a Solitary. I have accordingly aimed this book primarily at the Solitary Practitioner.

These Festivals are ancient, there is no doubt about that, but today, out of necessity, we often find we need to bring them in line with the parameters of modern life. Some of the practices and activities which would otherwise be impractical I have made more accessible by suggesting alternatives to traditional methods. Many of us no longer have access to open hearths and giant bonfires for example, so I have offered the alternatives I have found equally effective.

Life could be perilous for our ancestors and each festival marked a stepping stone from one seasonal change to the next.

Most of us no longer depend on the observance of the seasons to survive but the Wheel continues to turn and in doing so it demonstrate the astounding power of nature and its relentless progress. It reveals to us a power beyond our control yet one we can tap into. A power which is in the hands of the Divine. It instils in us a sense of awe and gratitude. For most, this gratitude expresses itself in the desire both to show appreciation and use that cosmic power to enrich not only our own lives but the world around us.

My hope is that these pamphlets will put your feet on the path of self-empowerment and instil a deeper appreciation of the staggering power of nature and the latent yet accessible power both within and around you. The Craft is not a 'dot to dot, follow my lead and do as I say' doctrine. It is a map. When you know the map and where to find what it is you need you can follow your chosen paths to it. Don't be told 'this way or no way'. Accept guidance, learn the routes then find your own way by your own self-empowerment.

Blessed Be.

Introduction

For the purposes of this pamphlet we will be celebrating the Goddess as the Triple Goddess - Maiden, Mother and Crone, as worshipped since the 7th millennium BC. And her Consort, the Lord of the Greenwood, in two of his guises, the Oak King and the Holly King. He is a God of fertility, growth, death and rebirth.

I have suggested spells and activities at the times of the year when the seasonal influences are particularly sympathetic to that particular intent. I have also suggested that some activities be performed during your ritual. They do not have to be performed within a Sabbat Ritual; indeed there are those who believe the Sabbat Ritual is solely to celebrate the Sabbat not for personal spells and undertakings. If you choose to keep the Sabbat ritual exclusively for the Sabbat then the spells and activities can be performed separately or within an Esbat (Full Moon) Ritual but preferably while the Elemental Tides, the influences of the Sabbat, are still active. They are at their height from midday the day before until midday the day after the Sabbat. Before and after that time they slowly diminish until the adjoining Sabbat influences begin to take effect. I have provided lists of correspondences for this festival. Correspondences are the colours, gems, herbs, incense, etcetera that are in tune with the season, your spell or your ritual's intent. For ease of use, and to allow you to select an alternative if you do not have the suggested item, I have included correspondence tables. With this you can link colour, gem stone, incense etcetera to the season or your spell. These are not meant to be exhaustive lists. There are many other choices available and no doubt you will add your own as you go.

Try not to get caught up on having just the right items, place, time, colour or any other of the endless conditions you think you need before you cast your spell or perform your ritual. Much of the power of your workings comes from your intent. Remember the old adage that *'if it be not found within then it be not found without'*. The power starts with you, the rest are aids, enhancements and focus items. See what works for you. Make notes then adapt and make more notes. Record which activities you chose to perform, the results of these activities and your thoughts, or suggestions, on how you can improve on it next time. <u>There are workbooks available here which are specifically designed</u> to work with 'The Wheel of the Year. *A beginners guide to celebrating the traditional pagan festivals of the year'*. They are perfect for creating your own Book of Shadows. The term 'Book of Shadows' simply refers to a record of things past; a shadow of all the activities you have performed and their results. It is particularly useful in allowing your power to grow and develop from your past experiences. It gives you your own personal guidelines as to what works for you. We are all unique.

When practising the Craft there is one major rule you should observe. It is known as the Witches Rede, sometimes known as the Wiccan Rede ('Wicca' believed to be derived from the ancient word for 'witch');

'If it harm none, do as you will.'

In the most basic of terms it seems to be saying you are free to do whatever you like. Sounds great! But it is not a licence to do as you want; it is a warning. It is reminding you that you must harm no-one and no-thing. And not just in the practising of the Craft. It is a pointer to a way of life. A moment's thought will show you that it can be far more difficult to follow the Witches Rede than at first glance; everything you do affects something or someone somewhere. You will do well to observe the guidance of the Rede however if for no other reason than whatever you send out will come back to you sooner or later. In the Wheel of the Year what goes around, comes around.

The Wheel of the Year
A short history

Most of the Festivals, or Sabbats, date back to pre-Christian times and all are linked to the changing of the seasons. The festivals marked a time to pause and reflect on what had gone before and a time to prepare for what was to come. The ability to understand and prepare for the relentless changing of the weather and cycles of crops and animals was essential. With the festivals our ancestors celebrated endings and new beginnings; the end of the earth's dormant period and the return of fertility culminating in successful harvests; followed once more by the end of summer and the return of shorter days, cold weather and the conserving and gathering of strength for the winter.

Although the festivals are ancient and mark important events in the cycle of the year the first known introduction of the year as a wheel was given to us by Ross Nicholls in the 1950s. The Wheel of the Year demonstrates the cycle of birth, death and rebirth in its never-ending journey. As the Wheel turns the Circle of Life is represented by the eight Festivals. They are divided into four Greater and four Lesser Sabbats, alternating about six weeks apart. The four Greater Sabbats, also called the Cross-Quarters, are based on pre-Christian festivals and are known as Fire Festivals. They are held on fixed days of the year. The four Lesser Sabbats, also called the Quarters, are celebrated on the two Equinoxes and two Solstices and so are based on the position of the sun.

Within the four Lesser Sabbats the two Equinoxes are Ostara (also known as the Spring Equinox) and Mabon (the Winter Equinox). 'Equi' translated from Latin is 'equal'. While 'nox' is 'night' so 'equal night' referring to the equal number of hours of daylight and darkness. The Equinoxes are by default opposite each other on the Wheel of the Year.

The two Solstices are Litha and Yule. The word Solstice translates to 'sun standing'. It refers to the sun's position in the sky at its northernmost or southernmost extreme due to the tilt of the Earth's axis being most inclined toward or away from the sun. So it is a time when the apparent movement of the sun comes to a stop before reversing direction. So at Litha we have the longest day and at Yule we have the shortest day. Again the two Solstices are opposite each other on the Wheel. These four Festivals divide the Wheel into Quarters.

The four Cross Quarters or Fire Festivals are the Greater Sabbats. They are pre-Christian and are based on cycles of life:-

    Samhain; represents endings and beginnings.
    Imbolc; a quickening.
    Beltain; fertility.
    Lammas, also known as Lughnasadh; harvest.

Each of these four Greater Sabbats is located midway between two Lesser Sabbats and at the turning points of the seasons. They cut across each quarter dividing the Wheel into eight parts. In this position these Sabbats look back to what was and look forward to what is to come.

It should be remembered that the eight festivals are attuned with the changing seasons of the year and so must change with where you are; the northern hemisphere being a direct opposite of the southern hemisphere. So though, for example, Beltain is celebrated on 1 May in the northern hemisphere, it is celebrated on 31 October in the southern hemisphere. I have given dates for both the northern and southern hemispheres. The southern hemisphere dates are in (brackets).

Festivals begin at sunset and last until the sunset of the next day.

Samhain - Greater Sabbat 31 October (1 May) - Root Harvest. Death and Rebirth. Communing with Ancestors. Cross Quarter. Fire Festival. Day of Power

Yule - Lesser Sabbat 20-21 December (21 June) - Winter Solstice. Return of the Oak King. Quarter. Longest night.

Imbolc - Greater Sabbat 1-2 February (2 August) - Purification. Quickening. Cross Quarter. Fire Festival. Day of Power.

Ostara - Lesser Sabbat 20-21 March (21 September) - Spring Equinox. Spring Goddess. Quarter. Equal day and night.

Beltain - Greater Sabbat 1 May (31 October) - Fertility. Cross

Quarter. Fire Festival. Day of Power.

Litha - Lesser Sabbat 20-21 June (21 December) - Summer Solstice. Return of the Holly King. Mid-summers Eve - offerings to the Fae. Quarter. Longest day.

Lammas - Greater Sabbat 1-2 August (2 February) - Bread Harvest. Cross Quarter. Fire festival. Day of Power.

Mabon - Lesser Sabbat 20-21 September (21 March) - Autumn Equinox, Vine Harvest. Quarter. Equal day and night.

Samhain
31 October (1 May)

Samhain, pronounced Sow-en, is a Cross-Quarter day midway between Mabon (the Autumn Equinox) and Yule (the Winter Solstice) and is one of the Greater Sabbats. It is both the end and the beginning of the Celtic and Wiccan year. It is often referred to as the Witch's New Year. Samhain is believed to be a Celtic word which, when loosely translated, means 'summers end'. This is a time when the third and final harvest is safely in and so it is appropriate to celebrate the fruitfulness of the land over the past year as it prepares to rest and regenerate through the winter.

This is also the time when the veil between the physical world and the world of Spirit is at its most insubstantial so it is a perfect time to remember and honour our ancestors.

The Goddess is now Crone. Today the title 'crone' often has unpleasant connotations, just as the word 'witch' does. In the context of the Goddess the word crone means, Wise Woman; One who holds knowledge. She and her consort have brought the world full circle. The God, still in the guise of the Holly King, is aging too. He is the Leader of the Wild Hunt and is often depicted with stag's antlers and in one last wild ride before he relinquishes his reign to the Oak King at Yule. The Holly King and the Oak King are two aspects of the same God.

Samhain is also known as Halloween of course. Around the 8th century the Catholic Church decided to use the first of November as All Saints Day; a day to honour all those saints without a day of their own. A Mass is said for them which is known as All Hallowmas, literally meaning 'a mass for all those who are hallowed'. The evening before the mass was known as Hallows Eve which over time became Halloween.

To our ancestors Samhain was the time to make preparations to survive the winter. Calculations were made as to how many beasts could be fed over the winter and which were to be slaughtered and the meat preserved to feed the family. The slaughter of the aged or surplus animals and the very fact that winter was such a perilous time for everyone, particularly the old, very young or sick, brought people face to face with the prospect of death. It is a theme which goes hand in hand with Samhain; new beginnings from the death of the old. It is death that gives life its sweetness and decay that feeds new life.

Today most of us no longer have that life and death struggle thankfully. But Samhain remains the time to take stock of our lives over the past year and plan for the new year. It is also the time to remember loved ones who are no longer with us and to ask for their blessings just as our ancestors did.

The Samhain Altar

Dress your Altar to honour this most magical of times with orange for new beginnings and black for endings. Or you can use silver and gold if you prefer. Autumn flowers, acorns, nuts, oak leaves, pomegranates, autumn leaves, apples - cut one across the centre to reveal the five pointed star within and smear it with lemon juice to keep it white. Miniature butternut squash and pumpkins will add colour. Cut some sage which represents wisdom and use for decoration and incense.

Suggested Activities for Samhain

Contacting your Ancestors
This is a powerful time for divination work and contacting the Spirit Realm because the veil between the two worlds is at its thinnest at Samhain. There are several ways to do this. I have outlined two; the Samhain feast and a meditation.

Seasonal Food for Your Feast
Roast vegetables. Beef, pork, poultry, black pudding and sausages. Pumpkin or butternut soups, broth, apples - try them stuffed with sweet mince and wrapped in flaky pastry or cut one in half across the middle to reveal the five pointed star at its heart. Smear it with lemon juice to keep it white. Also include nuts and anything from the last fruit harvest, pomegranates, potatoes, roasted pumpkin seeds and squash. Cider is a particularly appropriate drink or choose a red berry cordial or red wine.

The Samhain Feast
It is customary to hold a feast at Samhain. Bear in mind that this is the time the surplus farm animals were slaughtered and all the cuts which were not suitable to be preserved throughout the winter were to be used, not wasted. Our meal may not qualify as a feast today any more than a poor farmer's meal would have in past times but whatever its quantity and quality this is a meal which is shared with the departed. If possible use seasonal foods as the ancients would have; black pudding and beef, pork or poultry. Meat in the form of sausages is particularly appropriate as it is a way to use up scraps that would otherwise waste. Roast vegetables, pumpkin or butternut soups. Apples stuffed with sweet mince, toffee apples, nuts and anything from the last fruit harvest. Lay the table as usual but lay one more place than is needed, including a chair. This is for your Spirit guests. It is not necessary to lay more than one place for them. It is a symbolic welcoming and offering of sustenance. Put a little of what is on offer onto your guests' plate; make it attractive not just a mish-mash. Put a little of the red wine or red fruit juice in their glass. Invite them to come join you of their own free will and to depart freely at the end of the meal. Welcome them, speak to them. Leave pauses in the conversation to allow your own Spirit time to

hear what may be being said to it. It is a sober, respectful meal but not solemn. You are rejoicing in the attendance of your family and guides. Enjoy their company and be sure they know you appreciate their visit. At the end thank your guests for attending and visualize them returning to their own realm. The food which was offered to them can be taken out and offered to the wild animals or placed beneath a favourite tree with a blessing.

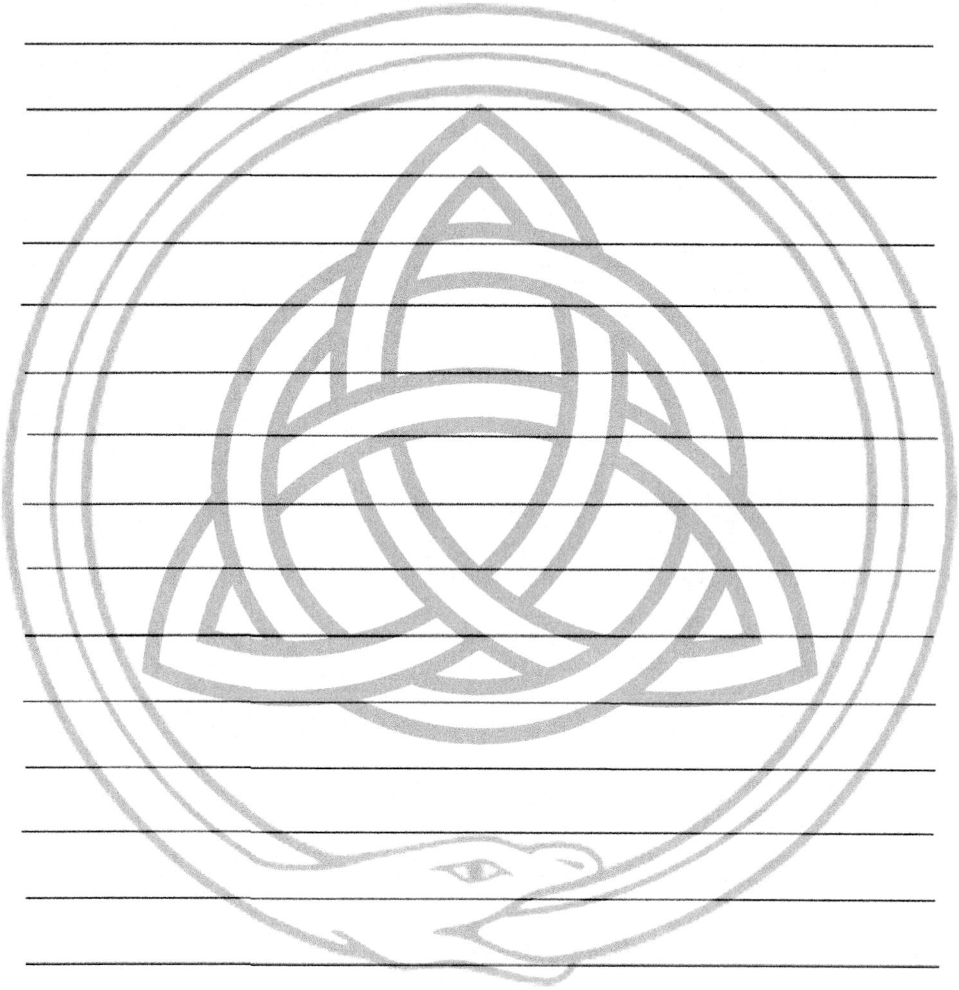

Samhain Correspondences

<u>Crystals and Gems</u>: Deep dark colours - dark jasper, onyx, sodalite or smoky quartz. And black gems such as obsidian and jet.
<u>Herbs</u>: Sage, thyme.
<u>Flora</u>: White flowers, fern, rose.
<u>Incense</u>: Myrrh, patchouli, dittany, sage, thyme.
<u>Colours</u>: Orange for ambition, success and new beginnings and black for endings and protection. Alternative colours are silver and gold.
<u>Element</u>: Air and Fire.
<u>Animals</u>: Raven, Blackbird, Goat, Dog, Wolf, Owl, Eagle.
<u>Tarot Card</u> - Death: Representing The Lord of Shadows and the Ending and Beginning aspect of Samhain.

Spells and Magical Workings for Samhain

To reflect the death and new life, endings and beginnings, which is the theme of Samhain magical workings at this time would ideally aim to replace the old with the seeds of future projects. Review what you have achieved or have not yet achieved over the past year. Plan to be rid of anything which is not serving you well such as bad habits, irrational fears, self-limiting attitudes or damaging relationships. Spells which bring about the ending of anything unwanted are particularly potent at this time.

These two spells rid you of the things you no longer want. They are best performed at midnight or midday. You do not need to cast a circle to perform them but if you are celebrating Samhain you could perform them before the cakes and wine and the opening of your circle.

Spell to Bring About an Ending
Items needed;
Small black candle.
Herb - sprig of rosemary and/or essential oil - frankincense.
Essential-oil warmer (if needed).
Old tin tray or tin lid.
Black pen.
Paper.

Arrange everything on your Altar or bench. Light the black candle and burn the herb, or heat the essential oil or use both if you prefer. When you are ready, if you have not already done so, light the black candle. Relax and find a state of calm. Then write what you want to be rid of on the paper and hold it to the flame saying, *'I sweep (name the thing) from my life'*. As it burns (over or in the tin tray for safety) visualize the thing being burned out of your life. Scatter the ashes in the wind and watch them blow away.

*****

Second Spell to End Something Unwanted
You will need;
A sigil you have previously practiced and charged. A sigil is a shape or design which is derived from a single word or simple phrase that outlines

your intent or desire. I have included a witch's sigil wheel for creating sigils with instructions on how to use it in part three of this book. For those who are reading this in eBook format or would simply like a full sized sigil wheel, there is a downloadable, full size sigil wheel on my blog at; http://maureen-murrish.blogspot.co.uk/
Small black candle.
Herb - rosemary and/or essential oil - frankincense.
Essential-oil warmer (if needed).
An orange stick, Boline, or sharp stick to inscribe the candle.

Arrange the items on your Altar or other suitable work surface. Inscribe the candle with the sigil. Sit back and watch the sigil and what it stands for dissolving out of your life as the candle burns. Visualise the habit or unwanted attention fading and finally disappearing. If possible choose a small candle that will burn fully then dispose of any remaining wax in the compost heap or garden waste recycling bin. Or, if you are using a chunky candle, mark or push a pin into the place you want it to burn to. Put the sigil above the mark. After the spell the candle can be stored and used for the same or similar purpose in the future.

*****

Spell to Empower New Ventures
This spell taps into the theme of new beginnings which is so powerful at Samhain. It will give your new goals or indeed long held goals an extra boost for success.
Items needed;
Orange, gold, green or white candle.
Essential oil - bay, cedar and/or cinnamon.
Herb - fennel, vervain and/or rosemary.
Pen and paper.
Essential-oil warmer (if needed)
Small pouch or paper bag to store some herbs and folded paper.

Light your coloured or white candle. Warm the essential oil or burn your herbs. Relax and when you are ready write down your goals. Be as exact or brief as you like and be positive. Your goals are achievable. Put them in the order you need to achieve them or in order of most desired result. Arrange them and rearrange them. When you have poured all your intentions onto your paper sit back and relax. Hold onto your paper and allow yourself to visualise your goals as achieved. Hang on to how that feels. Put the paper in a pouch with some of the herbs you used and store it with your magical tools or beneath an item on your Altar. Each month at the new moon bring it out, rewrite it if you wish omitting the goals you have achieved in the past month. Then visualise reaching your remaining goals.

*****

If you prefer more active pursuits how about getting out into the fresh air. Acknowledging and honouring festival does not always mean participating in formal rituals or spell work. A simple walk in the countryside can be equally stimulating. Notice the changes in the land, how it is preparing to sleep and regenerate for the coming year. You could work in the garden. Tidying and securing the plants and the ground for the winter is a good way to participate in the Samhain theme of endings and beginnings.

Samhain Meditation

A guide to meditation is included at part three of this book.
It may feel too intense if you hold your meditation on the same night as your feast if you are having one. In past times Samhain was spread over three days so it would be perfectly acceptable to conduct you mediation anytime from at noon of the 31st of October to noon of the 1st of November. If your meal has been a solitary feast where you have allowed all of your attention to remain on your otherworld guests it could be good now to make this a group activity, or vice versa.

Close your eyes and begin your mediation in the usual way with deep breaths and active relaxation. When you are ready visualize yourself in an open glade in a forest. Really put yourself there; listen to the noises, smell the air feel the breeze. Is it evening or day, are there lights? Music? You see an oak table which is decorated with flowers and herbs and set for a meal with your favourite seasonal foods. There are people around the table who smile and invite you to join them. Take the place laid ready for you. A lady at the head of the table stands and raises her arms. She says, 'On this night the veil between the worlds is gossamer-fine. We invite those who have passed beyond the veil to join our celebration for a while. Come of your own free will and enjoy good company and good cheer.'

Now you say, 'If you so will.' You do not need to say it aloud. In fact if you are in a group it would be very distracting for the others. But feel the words in your mind as if you were saying them.

Sit in silence for a few minutes and listen to the chatter. Then look around again and see who has joined the table. One by one welcome them and ask who they are. Listen to them, thank them for attending and speaking to you. What are they wearing? What do they look like? After ten minutes or so see them smile a farewell then walk away through the trees. Rise and take your leave of the dinner party. Thanking them for having you. When you are ready return to the room you are sitting in. Give yourself a few minutes to return fully then eat your snack and drink your fruit juice or tea while you write in your journal any messages and impressions or pictures you gained.

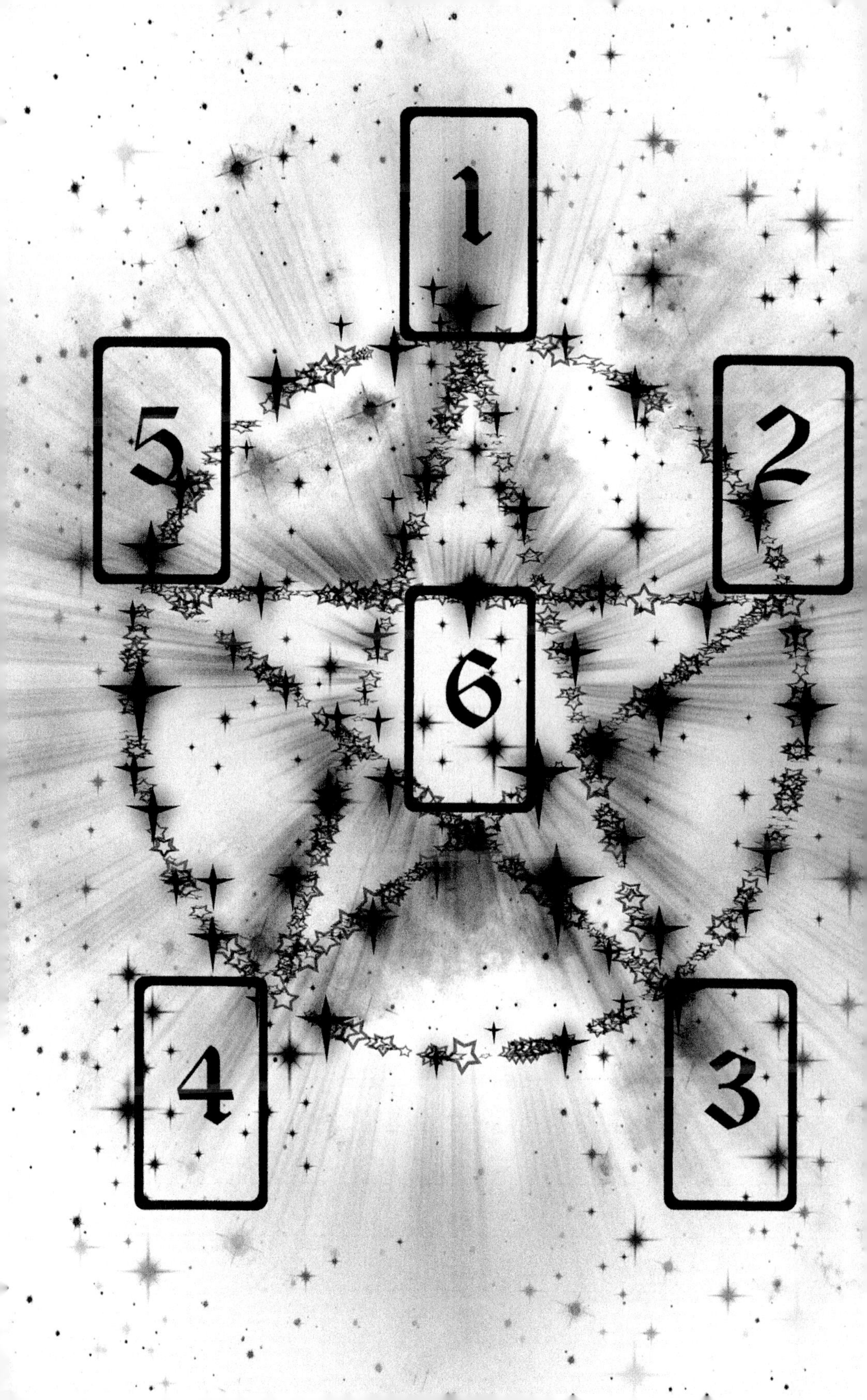
1
2
3
4
5
6

Samhain
Tarot Spread

1. What area should I focus on growing in this New Year?

2. What is holding me back that I need to be rid of?

3. How can I strengthen my spirituality?

4. How can I forge stronger personal relationships.

5. What can I expect between Samhain and Yule?

6. What wisdom would my ancestors like to offer me?

Butternut Squash Soup

Ingredients
1 butternut squash, about 1kg, peeled and deseeded
2 tbsp olive oil
1 tbsp butter
2 onions diced
1 garlic clove, thinly sliced
2 mild red chillies, deseeded and finely chopped
850ml hot vegetable stock
4 tbsp crème fraîche, plus more to serve

Method
1. Heat oven to 200C/180C fan/gas 6.
2. Cut 1 peeled and deseeded butternut squash into large cubes, about 4cm/1½in across, then toss in a large roasting tin with 1 tbsp of the olive oil.
3. Roast for 30 mins, turning once during cooking, until golden and soft.
4. While the butternut squash cooks, melt 1 tbsp butter with the remaining 1 tbsp olive oil in a large saucepan, then add 2 diced onions, 1 thinly sliced garlic clove and ¾ of the 2 deseeded and finely chopped red chillies.
5. Cover and cook on a very low heat for 15-20 mins until the onions are completely soft.
6. Tip the butternut squash into the pan, add 850ml hot vegetable stock and 4 tbsp crème fraîche, then whiz with a stick blender until smooth. For a really silky soup, put the soup into a liquidiser and blitz it in batches.
7. Return to the pan, gently reheat, then season to taste.
8. Serve the soup in bowls with swirls of crème fraîche and a scattering of the remaining chopped chilli.

Recipe from Good Food Magazine

Herb Pouch

Psychic Awareness

This is a herb recipe to aid your psychic awareness. You need to carry it with you and have it beneath your pillow for a full luna month. Wrap the herbs in a violet coloured cloth tied up with a silver cord.

When preparing these recipes chose a time when you are calm and not likely to be interrupted. Perhaps after a meditation or after a soothing walk in the garden or countryside. If you are using fresh ingredients perhaps you could gather them while walking, all but the cinnamon that is! Concentrate on the purpose of your gathering. While assembling the pouch focus on the result you desire.

Half a stick of cinnamon
A bay leaf. Dried or fresh
A Peppermint leaf. (I find fresh mint leaves from the garden work very well too)
Fresh or dried Rosemary
Fresh or dried Thyme

Other books by M Murrish:-
Work books:
The Wheel of the Year: *A beginners guide to celebrating the traditional pagan festivals of the seasons.*

The Wheel of the Year: *A 1yr 3yr or 5 year work book and Journal for the pagan festivals. (Companion workbook to: A beginners guide to celebrating the traditional pagan festivals of the seasons.)*

Three Card Spread Tarot Journal: *Ideas for three card spreads including prompts with room for your detailed interpretation and outcome.*

I AM....: *A prompted motivational affirmation journal to increase self-esteem and self empowerment*

Family Tree Research Journal: *Family history fill-in charts and research forms in a handy and logically ordered workbook*

Weaving Project Planner and Journal: *Designed for the beginner or experienced weaver working on a rigid heddle, 4 or 8 shaft loom.*

Gardening Journal Monthly Planner: *Organise your garden week by week with detailed record sheets and a diary based log book.*

Novels:
The Bonding Crystal: *book one of the Dragon World Series. A fantasy adventure with dragons, sorcery, elves and goblins.*

The Missing Link: *book two of the Dragon World Series.*

The Forth Gate: *book three of the Dragon World Series.*

The Lost Sorcerer: *A novella*

Thank you for choosing this Journal. If you find it as useful and inspiring as we do please consider leaving a positive review on Amazon as it will help others to find it too.

Scan the QR code below to check out our other books, notebooks, journals and reference books.

https://maureenmurrish.com

Printed in Great Britain
by Amazon